The Sun

Ray Spangenburg and Kit Moser

Watts LIBRARY

Franklin Watts
A Division of Scholastic Inc.
New York • Toronto • London • Auckland • Sydney
Mexico City • New Delhi • Hong Kong
Danbury, Connecticut

Note to readers: Definitions for words in **bold** can be found in the Glossary at the back of this book.

Photographs ©: Art Resource, NY: 8 (SEF); Bridgeman Art Library International Ltd., London/New York: 17 (BL 22556/British Library, London, UK), 46 (MOL 5332/Museum of London, UK); Corbis-Bettmann: 14 (Paul Almasy), 3 top, 9, 12; Holiday Film Corp: 26; Liaison Agency, Inc.: 17 inset (Roger Viollet); NASA: 50 (Howard Bond/STScl), 39 (GSFC), 34, 38; Photo Researchers, NY: 49 (John Chumack), 22 (David Hardy/SPL), 3 bottom, 6, 7 (Chris Butler/SPL), 11 (SPL) 29 (NASA/SPL), 32 (Rev. Ronald Royer/SPL), 37 (Jack Finch/SPL), 42 (Ton Kinsbergen/SPL), 47 (UK Meteorological Office/SPL); SOHO: 25 (ESA/NASA), 44 (NASA); The Planetarium: 4 (Anglo-Australian Telescope Board), 30, 40 (NASA/JPL), Tom Stack & Associates: cover (NOAA/TSADO).

Solar system diagram created by Greg Harris

Library of Congress Cataloging-in-Publication Data

Spangenburg, Ray, 1939–
    The sun / Ray Spangenburg and Kit Moser.
        p.   cm.— (Watts Library)
    Includes bibliographical references and index.
    ISBN 0-531-11767-7 (lib. bdg.)   0-531-13991-3 (pbk.)
    1. Sun—Juvenile literature. [1. Sun.] I. Moser, Diane, 1944– II. Title. III. Series.
QB521.5 .S73 2001
523.7—dc21   00-039924

GROLIER
PUBLISHING
1 2 3 4 5 6 7 8 9 10 R 10 09 08 07 06 05 04 03 02 01

Contents

The Sun took form in a huge, glowing cloud of dust and gas.

Chapter One

Our Star, the Sun

The story of the Sun first began about 4.5 billion years ago. It all started when bits of dust and hot gases in space began to form a huge cloud known as the **solar nebula**. Slowly, the force of **gravity** pulled these cloud particles toward each other. Eventually, the particles were packed so close that the cloud began to contract, or shrink. A very young star—a **protostar**—was formed.

This young star created a large amount of pressure as its **mass** continued to push

Just One of the Gang

To the observer on Earth, our Sun seems much bigger than any other star. This is because our Sun is so close and other stars are so far away. When compared to these distant stars, our Sun is an average size. It is classified as a dwarf star.

There are many stars that are smaller than the Sun and there are a few large stars that have diameters a thousand times bigger than the Sun's, but most stars in the universe are about the same size as the Sun.

A solar system (red disk) begins to form around a star.

inward. This inward pressure produced heat. The new star's temperature rose steadily and it began to shine. Finally, this protostar's center became hot enough to give off great amounts of energy, and our Sun was born.

As the Sun formed, a huge, hot mass of gases and dust continued to swirl around it. Slowly, the gases and dust began to cool off and clump together. These clumps attracted more material, and soon they formed larger masses. Finally, the

clumps formed into larger and larger balls of rock and gas. These worlds became the planets and their moons, along with **asteroids**, **comets**, and meteoroids, all **orbiting** the Sun.

The Sun is very important to life on Earth. The Sun's light and warmth make our crops grow and our forests flourish. Without the Sun, Earth would have no day, no night, and no seasons. There would be no food to eat. No life would be able to exist on Earth without the Sun.

Ancient peoples knew how important the Sun was. In many ancient cultures, the Sun was considered a god. The ancient Maya

This ancient temple was built in eastern India between 1238 and 1264 and was dedicated to Surya, god of the Sun.

in southern Mexico built temples where they worshiped the Sun. In Hindu mythology, the Sun god's name is Surya. Ancient Egyptians called the Sun god Amon-Re, or Amon-Ra. In ancient Greece, the Sun god's name was Helios. The Greeks believed Helios drove a horse-drawn chariot across the sky every day. Early American Indian nations held special ceremonies and dances to honor the Sun. Many ancient peoples made offerings and performed rituals. They hoped to persuade the powerful Sun god to be kind and bring plentiful crops.

Many early cultures built observatories that also served as places of worship. Stonehenge in England is one of the most famous. It was built at about the same time as the pyramids in Egypt. The thirty tall stones of Stonehenge form a huge circle of pillars, and great connecting stones are laid across the tops. An altar stone resides within the circle. A tall, pointed "heel stone" stands at the entrance. At sunrise on the first day of summer, the Sun aligns directly with the huge heel stone as seen from inside the great stone circle. Clearly, Stonehenge is a monument built to help record and observe such special solar events as the first day of summer and the first day of winter. However, researchers are not sure exactly how the

prehistoric builders used Stonehenge. Many similar sites were constructed all over the world by ancient peoples—including American Indians. Solar events played a universally important role in human lives everywhere.

Solar Eclipses

People noticed that sometimes a giant, dark, round shadow covered the Sun. To early humans, the darkened daytime sky must have been frightening. Suddenly in the middle of the day it became dark enough to see the stars and planets. Some ancients thought this event was a warning. Perhaps a disaster, such as a flood or avalanche, was coming. Perhaps a ruler was

Stonehenge is an ancient monument built of huge upright stones. Monuments were built on this site as long ago as ca. 2950 B.C. This stone version of the monument was constructed between ca. 2100 and 1600 B.C.

about to die or be overthrown. Perhaps an invisible dragon was trying to take a bite out of the Sun. As long ago as 2137 B.C., predicting this event was an important job in China. The Chinese tried to frighten the dragon away by making a lot of noise with drums, pans, or anything that was handy. In India, people performed a ritual of dipping themselves into water neck-high to encourage peace between the dragon and the Sun and Moon. Native Americans in the Arctic regions—including the Tlingits, Eskimos, and Aleuts—believed that during an eclipse the Sun and the Moon left their places in the sky and came down to Earth to see how things were going.

Of course, we now know that this event is a natural occurrence called an eclipse. It is the Moon, not a dragon, that blocks out the Sun's light. As the Moon **revolves** around Earth, there are times when it passes directly in front of the Sun and blocks the Sun's light. Even though the Moon is much smaller than the Sun, it can still completely hide the Sun during an eclipse as we watch from Earth. This is possible because the Moon is much closer to Earth than the Sun

Viewing the Sun Safely

Never look directly at the Sun, even during an eclipse. Its intense light can instantly and permanently damage your eyes. Don't use binoculars or a telescope, either—not even on a cloudy day, and not even at sunset or sunrise.

If you ever want to watch an eclipse, here is a safe way to "see" the Sun: Place a piece of black paper with a pinhole in it over a mirror and shine the Sun's reflection on a wall or the side of a building.

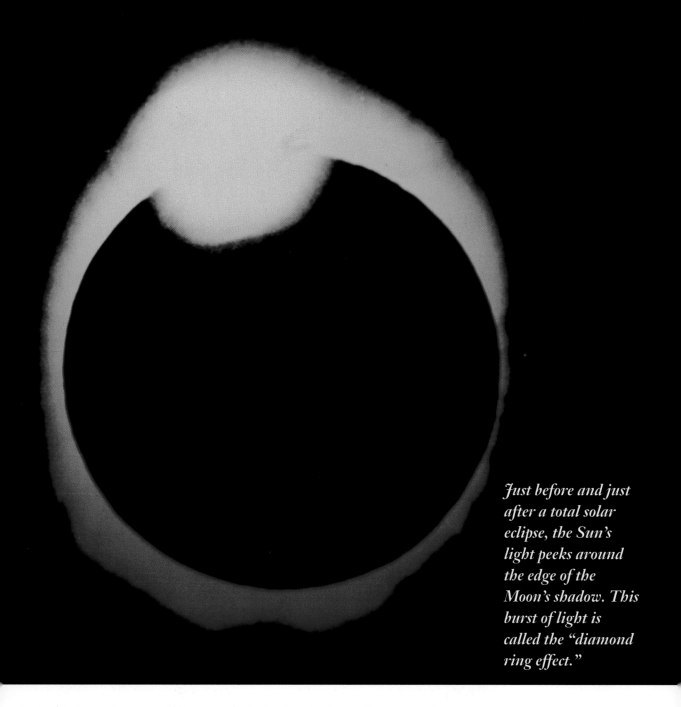

Just before and just after a total solar eclipse, the Sun's light peeks around the edge of the Moon's shadow. This burst of light is called the "diamond ring effect."

is. The Sun is 93 million miles (150 million kilometers) away from Earth while the Moon is 238,860 miles (384,407 km) away from Earth.

To the observer on Earth, the Sun seems to move across the sky, but it is really Earth that is moving.

Chapter Two

Center Stage

As you stand on our planet's surface, you probably feel as though you are standing still. The Sun seems to be traveling across the sky. It rises from the horizon in the east and sets in the west. Actually, though, it is Earth that is moving, not the Sun.

Earth turns, or **rotates**, around an imaginary line, or **axis**, that runs from north to south through its poles. One full turn, or rotation, takes Earth one full day (24 hours) to complete. As the planet rotates, different regions face the Sun. Earth turns one side toward the Sun at a time. One side is in daylight while the other side is in darkness. As the planet turns, daylight moves westward. In one 24-hour period, any one place on Earth enjoys about half the time in sunlight, or daytime. The other 12 hours are spent facing away from the Sun, toward the darkness of space. So, Earth is actually spinning, and you are going along for the ride!

Long ago, people used Earth's rotation to tell time. For millennia, people used sundials instead of clocks. A sundial is one of the earliest scientific instruments. Its indicator juts up from the center, positioned to cast a shadow on the markings

This sundial, built in Poland in the 1700s, is still in use after more than 200 years. People tell time based on the position of the Sun's shadow.

of a surrounding dial. The dial's markings represent the hours of a day. As Earth rotates, the position of the Sun changes in the sky, so the angle of the shadow changes. From hour to hour the shadow falls across different markings around the dial, just as an hour hand points to different numbers on a modern-day clock.

The Sun at the Center

Besides rotating on its axis, Earth also travels in an orbit—or revolves—around the Sun. One revolution around the Sun takes 365 days, or one solar year. Astronomers in some cultures understood this arrangement, but until the mid-1500s, most European scientists based their view of the universe on the ideas of ancient Greek philosophers, including Aristotle (384–322 B.C.). The Greek philosophers thought the Sun and all the other spheres in the sky revolved in perfect circles around Earth—an idea known as the geocentric solar system ("geo-" meaning "earth" and "-centric" meaning "centered").

The geocentric view had a few problems, though. Some things just didn't work right. Astronomers had noticed for a long time that Mars did not always move in a straight line. Instead, it seemed to stop and then double back! What could cause such strange behavior? One idea was that Mars made little loops as it moved in its orbit around Earth. Even this idea did not really explain the odd movements of Mars.

Then a Polish mathematician and astronomer named Nicolaus Copernicus began to work on a different idea. He studied the skies night after night and made some calculations. If Mars orbited the Sun, not Earth, that difference would explain the way Mars looked when it crossed the nighttime sky. He realized that the same solution would solve similar problems for other planets. Copernicus concluded that the Sun—not Earth—is the center of our solar system. In 1543, he published a book about this revolutionary idea, known as the heliocentric solar system ("helio" means "Sun"). For European science, his book began an important new way of thinking about the Sun and the solar system.

It's All in the Tilt

Depending on where you live, you may know what a large effect the changing seasons can have on human lives. They affect the growing season—how long plants can grow and produce, and during what time of year. They may affect the type of shelter you need and the clothes you wear. They influence how and where you spend your time—outside or inside, in a

Nicolaus Copernicus (1473–1543) suggested that the solar system is heliocentric, or Sun-centered. This diagram from the seventeenth century illustrates the system Copernicus devised.

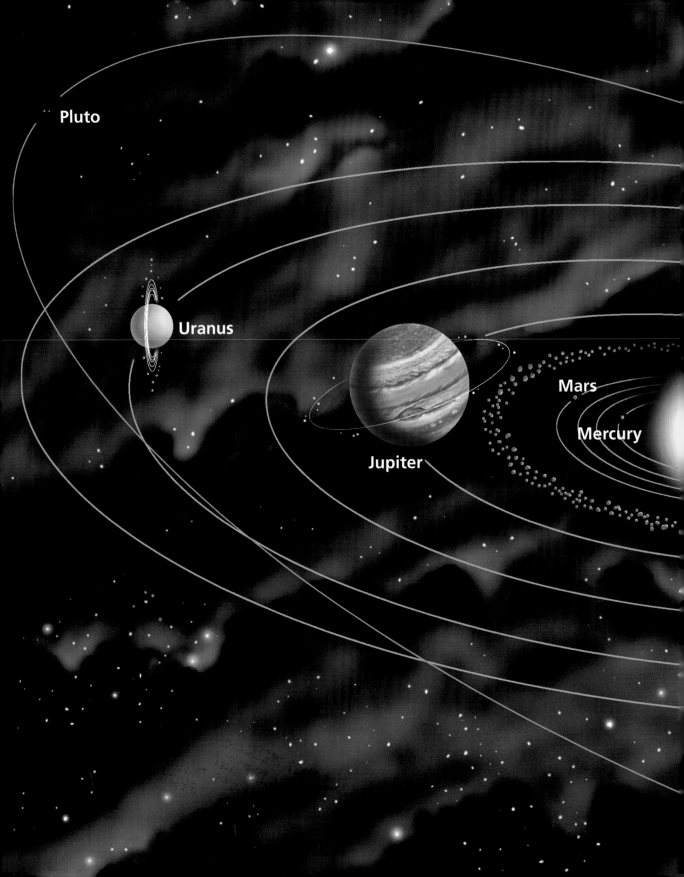

The Solar System

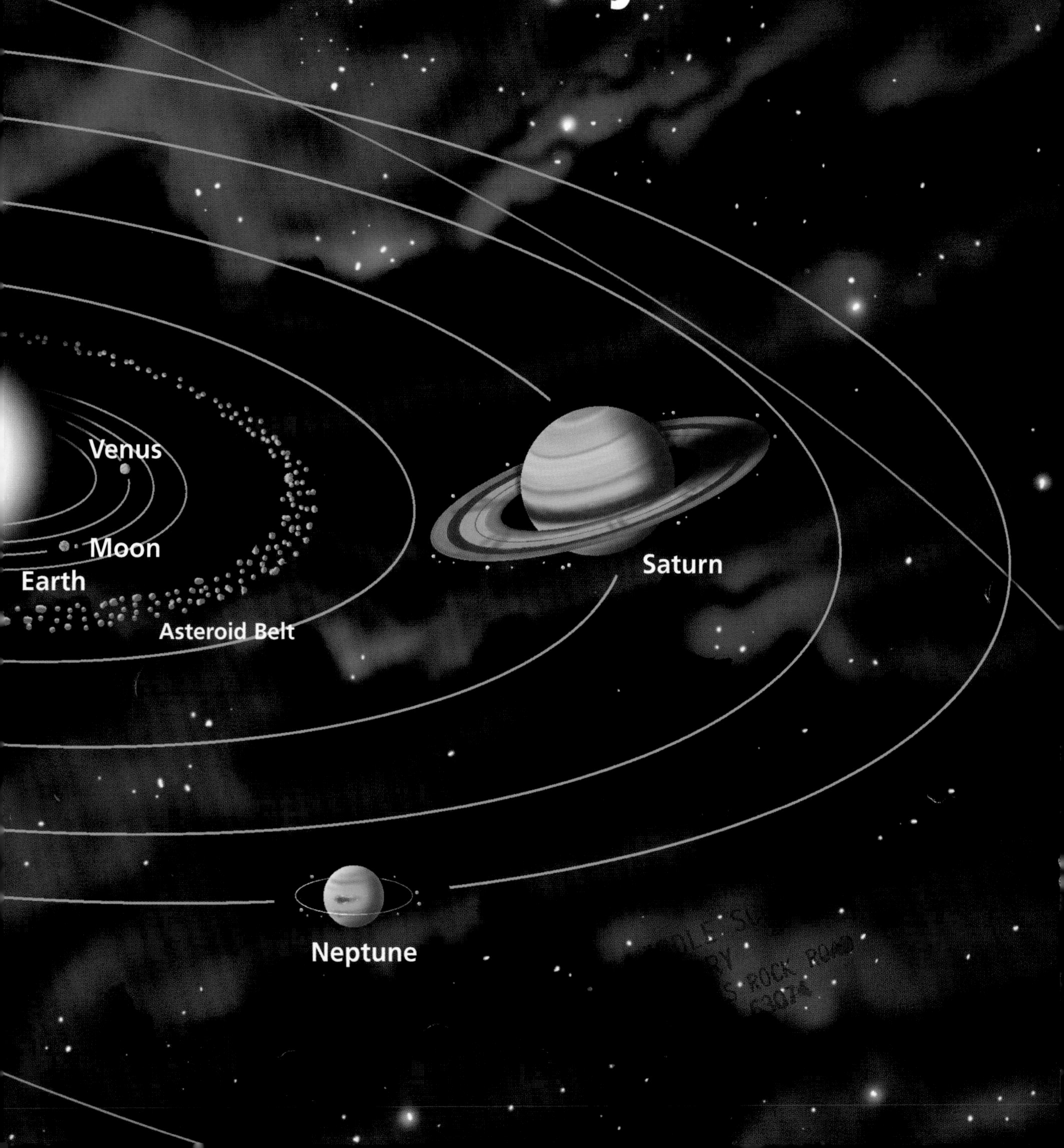

Venus

Moon

Earth

Asteroid Belt

Saturn

Neptune

Earth is tipped on its axis as it orbits the Sun. As shown in this drawing, the Northern Hemisphere is tilted toward the Sun's warmth and light. As Earth continues to revolve, the Southern Hemisphere will eventually be tilted toward the Sun.

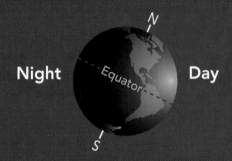

Night   Day

swimming pool or skiing down a mountainside. Contrary to ideas that are popular even today, though, the seasons are not caused by how close the Sun is to Earth—at least not completely. Earth does travel in an ellipse and sometimes the Sun is farther away than at other times. However, the temperature difference caused by Earth's orbit is slight. The tilt in the Earth's axis is the main cause of the seasons.

As Earth spins on its axis, this imaginary line is not straight up and down. It is tilted about 23.5 degrees. That's not a lot, but it is enough so the Northern and Southern Hemispheres receive different amounts of sunlight at different times of the year. Also, the Sun sometimes shines directly down on a region, and sometimes it angles through the layers of Earth's **atmosphere**. The Sun is Earth's only source of light, energy, and heat. Any change in the amount of light that hits Earth will have a direct effect on the weather. When the amount of sunlight an area receives changes over a period of time, that area experiences different seasons—winter, spring, summer, and fall.

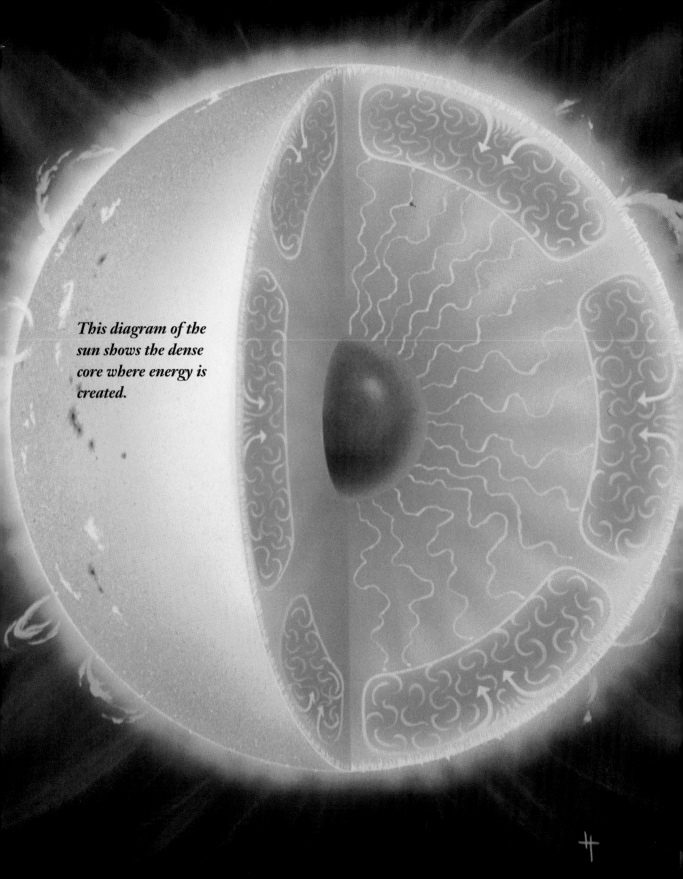

This diagram of the sun shows the dense core where energy is created.

Chapter Three

The Sun's Composition

The Sun's energy is produced in its **core** by a process called **nuclear fusion**. The Sun is mostly composed of a gas called hydrogen. Like everything else in the universe, hydrogen is composed of tiny particles called **atoms**. The enormous weight of the Sun's outer layers presses constantly inward. So, the atoms of the Sun's core are very close together. As the atoms move about constantly, they collide with each other and split apart. The separated atoms move very fast because of the heat and pressure in the core. They slam into each other and fuse together, or combine, to form another gas called helium. Whenever this fusion occurs, a tiny amount of matter is converted to energy. The Sun creates 4 million tons of energy every second. Looking at it another way, each ounce of matter converted to energy through fusion would keep a 100-watt lightbulb burning for about 750,000 years. That's a lot of energy!

The Sun's energy travels in packets called **photons** and reaches us in the form of sunlight. A photon has no mass, and it may exist for an extremely long time. Each photon begins its journey in the Sun's core and then passes through the many layers of the Sun before it journeys to Earth. Finding its way to the outer layer of the Sun is not easy, as it bounces from atom to atom through the densely packed core and then in the zone above it called the **radiative zone**. It can take as long as a million years for a photon to find its way out.

Even then, a photon is not ready to take off to carry sunlight to Earth and the other planets. The photon passes next through another zone, called the **convective zone**. Here a process called convection moves hot gases upward and outward through the layer like water boiling in a pot. Hot gases bubble upward to the surface. The process continues as the gases cool, sink downward, heat up, and rise again, until the energy finally escapes.

Finally, the photon reaches the **photosphere**, where smaller convection cells bubble energy up to the surface. Once

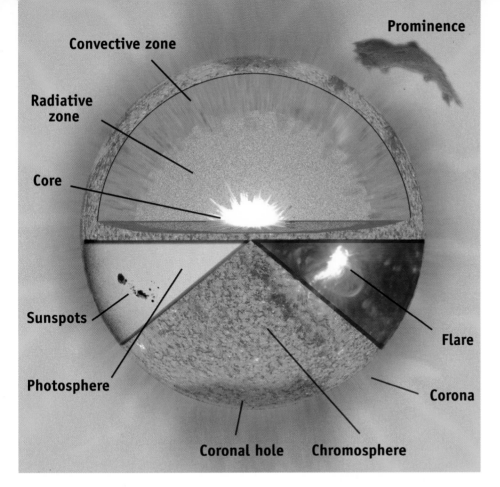

Prominence

Convective zone

Radiative zone

Core

Sunspots

Photosphere

Coronal hole

Chromosphere

Flare

Corona

This overview diagram shows the Sun's parts and a few of its many kinds of activity.

at the photosphere the photon's trip speeds up. From the edge of the photosphere to Earth, sunlight can make the trip in just a little over 8 minutes!

The Sun's Surface

Even though the photosphere is composed of gas, it is sometimes called the Sun's surface because it is the outermost layer that you see in pictures. This is the layer where sunspots—slightly cooler, darker areas of the Sun—can be seen. Also, masses of bright gases burst from the photosphere into the Sun's atmosphere, creating huge arcs.

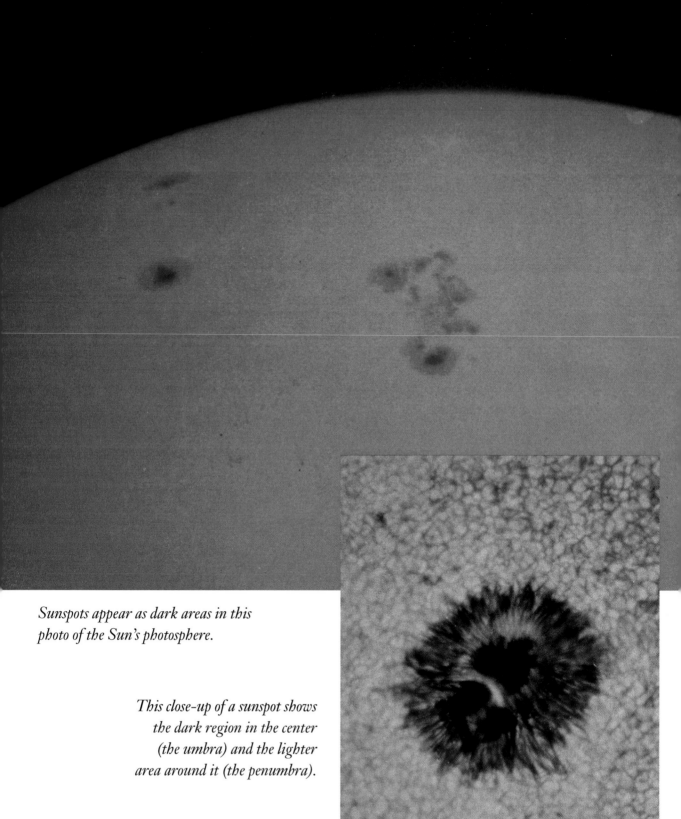

Sunspots appear as dark areas in this
photo of the Sun's photosphere.

This close-up of a sunspot shows
the dark region in the center
(the umbra) and the lighter
area around it (the penumbra).

Greek philosophers thought the Sun and all the spheres of the solar system were perfect in every way. So, astronomers had a hard time explaining sunspots. They concluded that the sunspots were near the Sun, not on it. Then, around 1611, the Italian scientist Galileo Galilei found a way to study these spots firsthand. He projected the Sun's image through his telescope onto a paper screen and sketched the spots he saw for several days. From his sketches, he could see that from one day to the next, the sunspots appeared in different positions. That meant they had to be on the Sun and that the Sun must be moving. Galileo concluded that the Sun rotates on an axis, much as Earth does.

Scientists now know that sunspots can interfere with satellite transmissions, electrical power service, and other areas of human life on Earth 93 million miles (150 million km) away. Scientists know that sunspots have huge concentrations of **magnetism**, an often powerful force possessed by magnets. Refrigerator magnets use the force of magnetism. The magnet is attracted to the steel door of the refrigerator. This attraction creates enough force to hold the two objects together, so the magnet sticks to the refrigerator. Sometimes screwdrivers are magnetized to hold metal screws in place as they are screwed. The area around the magnetic object that is affected by its magnetism is called a **magnetic field**.

You can think of the Sun as an enormous magnet. This magnet is so strong that it can attract and repel objects even when it is not in direct contact with them. Its magnetic fields

How a Magnet Works

You can see a magnetic field at work by trying a simple experiment. You'll need a strong bar magnet, a piece of paper, and a handful of iron filings. Place the bar magnet on a table and sprinkle the iron filings on the paper. Then hold the paper just over the magnet and tap the paper. The filings rearrange themselves! It looks like magic, but it is actually nature at work. Clusters of filings collect around each pole (at each end of the bar). The rest arrange themselves in lines that form half-circles from pole to pole. The midpoint in each half circle has fewer filings, and most of the filings collect where the lines of force are strongest, at the poles. The lines you see are magnetic field lines, showing the path the filings follow as they are being pulled toward the poles.

play important roles in the violent activity that takes place there. Sunspots are caused when powerful magnetic forces slow down the movement of atoms. These forces travel along lines of magnetism that usually run from the north pole of the Sun to the south pole. Since the Sun is not solid, as it rotates some of the Sun's gases rotate faster than others—especially near the Sun's **equator**. When this happens, these invisible magnetic lines become twisted, and they sometimes poke through the surface, causing slower motion and cooler regions. These are the darker, cooler areas we call sunspots. Some sunspots are so large they could engulf Earth. A closer look has revealed that two areas are visible in many larger spots—a dark region called the umbra, and a lighter region called the penumbra.

Sunspots are not the only areas of activity on the photos-

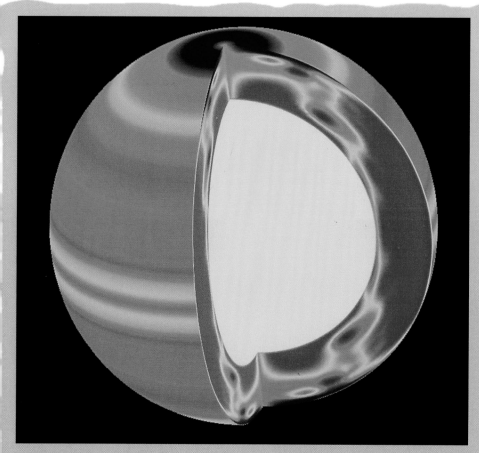

Different Speeds

Have you ever stirred a can of paint? As you swirl the stick, the paint at the center of the can may move faster than the paint near the edges. The Sun's gases also move at different speeds, depending on their location. In this colored image of the Sun, the red and yellow areas move faster than the blue and green areas.

phere. Huge, immensely hot, glowing gases burst through the photosphere into the upper layers of the Sun. These bursts, called prominences, often loop and double-loop back on themselves. Sometimes, these brightly glowing particles will break loose and catapult wildly away from the surface of the Sun. Astronomers call this kind of energy burst an "eruptive prominence." At other times, gases break away and fall toward the Sun.

Sometimes, these huge clouds of solar gas may be held by the Sun's magnetic field high above the surface. This type of solar prominence may stay in place for several hours or even

Earth would look tiny in comparison to many of the Sun's huge eruptive prominences as they hurl hot gases into space.

SIZE OF EARTH

several days. Its arch may be so high that our entire planet Earth could fit between its loop and the surface of the Sun.

The Sun's Atmosphere

Just above the photosphere astronomers have detected a thin, rosy layer of gas. This layer is known as the **chromosphere** (or "color sphere") because of this rosy color. It can be seen during a solar eclipse, when the moon blocks the Sun's light. Its thin, red or rose-colored outline surrounds the Moon's dark, circular disk as the Moon slips in front of the Sun. The temperature of the chromosphere is cooler at the inside edge than at the outside edge. On the inside edge, near the photosphere, the temperature can be as low as 7,600 degrees Fahrenheit (4,200 degrees Celsius). As the chromosphere's gases move toward the coolness of space, they become almost twice as hot, reaching temperatures as high as 14,800° F (8,200° C). This fact has puzzled scientists, as it would make more sense for the areas closer to the heated core of the Sun to be hotter. In the transition zone, between the photosphere and the chromosphere, scientists have spotted clustered jets of hot gas, called spicules, that spike upward in short spurts. These gases jump from the photosphere to the chromosphere. Scientists think these spicules may be responsible for the strangely extreme heat that bubbles up to the surface of the chromosphere.

The outermost layer is the **corona** (or "crown"). This is perhaps the most beautiful portion of the Sun. Ancient

*the photosphere is
blocked from view.*

The Sun at a Glance

Diameter	864,327 miles (1.39 million km)
Mass	2.2 thousand trillion trillion tons
Average Density	1.41 times the density of water
Temperature at the Surface	10,142° F (5,617° C)
Temperature at the Core	27 million° F (15 million° C)
Average Distance from Earth	93 million miles (150 million km)
Age	4.5 billion years

astronomers knew the Sun has a halo of bright light that extends far beyond the bright ball of gas we normally see. They had seen the corona during solar eclipses, when the Moon blocks out the Sun. The corona's pale white glow and its broad, jagged spikes reach millions of miles into space. This outermost layer of the Sun's atmosphere reaches temperatures as high as 1.8 million° F (1 million° C). This is much higher than the layer below. As with the chromosphere, scientists have been trying for years to find out why this outermost layer is so much hotter than anyone expected.

In this colorful picture taken onboard Skylab, *the corona is color coded to show the different levels of brightness.*

Chapter Four

The Sun's Vast Outreach

Since it is dangerous to look directly at the Sun, photographs are important in helping scientists to observe our star. In the 1970s, the United States launched *Skylab*. The astronauts that staffed this space station from 1973 to 1974 took more than 30,000 photographs of the Sun from space. These pictures provide keys that allow scientists to understand the direct effects the Sun has on Earth, from interruptions in radio signals to the beautiful Northern Lights. Space-based missions in the last half of the twentieth century began to open up exciting new levels of understanding of the Sun's inner processes that were not possible using even the most powerful Earth-based telescopes.

Solar Wind

When the different layers of gases in the Sun rotate, the Sun's magnetic field twists with them. When the magnetic field is twisted enough, it breaks and the force cuts holes in the Sun's corona. A hot flow of charged particles called the **solar wind** escapes through these holes into space. The solar wind flows faster than sound, at speeds as high as 1.6 million miles (2.58 million km) per hour. It engulfs the entire system of planets, moons, asteroids, and comets that we call the solar system. On Earth, you may sometimes see the effect of the solar wind in the beautiful displays of nighttime color known as the **aurora borealis**. This stunning light show, also known as the Northern Lights, occurs near the North Pole. A similar display, called the aurora australis, occurs in the regions near the South Pole. Colored streams of light dance across the skies, putting on a beautiful show. Scientists now think this display is caused by the interaction of the solar wind's charged particles and molecules in Earth's atmosphere. Earth's own magnetic field directs the magnetic particles of the solar wind into Earth's atmosphere.

The solar wind can cause problems on Earth, though. Its radiation can interfere with electrical and radio transmissions.

Astronauts may risk exposure to high levels of radiation when the solar wind increases, and even fliers in high-altitude aircraft face a tiny risk from the intense radiation.

Scientists are so interested in the solar wind that most scientific satellites and spacecraft carry instruments to study it—even if the main mission is something different. Spacecraft have studied the far-reaching effects of the solar wind at all the planets except Pluto.

Interaction between the solar wind and Earth's upper atmosphere causes an awe-inspiring light show called the aurora borealis.

Solar Flares

Among the most impressive occurrences that spacecraft have photographed on the Sun are **solar flares**. These bursts of light and energy at the Sun's surface are the most energetic explosions in the solar system. If we could harness the energy of just one solar flare, it would provide enough electricity to power everything that anyone on Earth might need for millions of years.

The *Solar Maximum Mission* (*Solar Max* or *SMM*) was launched in 1980 to study solar flares and the Sun's atmosphere. Its mission was to study the Sun during its most active period, but a problem developed that interrupted the mission.

Astronauts took this photo of Solar Max *as they prepared to send it back into space.*

Spacecraft Engineer

Aprille Ericsson-Jackson began life in a poor New York neighborhood. She worked hard at what she loved and went on to study engineering at Massachusetts Institute of Technology (MIT) and earned a Ph.D. at Howard University in Washington, D.C. Recently, as an aerospace engineer for NASA, Ericsson-Jackson helped design *TRACE* (*Transition Region and Coronal Explorer*), a mission to study solar flares and prominences.

In 1984, astronauts aboard the space shuttle *Challenger* rescued the spacecraft and repaired it. *Solar Max* continued to study the Sun for another 5 years. *Yohkoh*, which means "sunbeam" in Japanese, was launched a year later, in 1991, by Japan. It is designed to study solar flares in the corona by detecting high energy X-ray and gamma-ray radiation.

One of NASA's spacecraft, the *Transition Region and Coronal Explorer* (*TRACE*), was launched in 1998. It began its study of the Sun's upper atmosphere in 1999. It is designed to study solar flares and other processes of the Sun.

This photo taken by Solar Max shows the Sun's corona extending into space.

Scientists have learned that solar flares send intense radiation far into space. As the solar wind swoops past Earth, it carries the flare's highly charged particles. A flare's radiation takes 8 minutes to travel from the Sun to Earth. When it arrives, Earth's upper atmosphere becomes electrically charged and expands. Changes in the upper atmosphere can affect long-distance radio signals. Satellites can be dragged out of their orbits by the expanded atmosphere. Electronic components onboard satellites and even electrical devices on Earth can be damaged.

One explanation for solar flares is that the magnetic field lines on the outer edges of the Sun's photosphere become twisted, as if you were twisting rubber bands. This may happen because the Sun's gases rotate at different speeds in different regions. Tension builds up as the lines get twisted tighter and the movement of gas atoms is restricted. Then, finally, something snaps. The release of the restraints produces a huge explosion. It would be very helpful to us on Earth if observations of changes in the Sun's magnetic fields could help predict flares. So far, though, attempts at predictions have not been very successful.

Maximum Observation

Scientists knew that a time called Solar Maximum was coming up around the year 2001. During a Solar Maximum, sunspots and other activity on the Sun take place in much greater numbers. The National Aeronautics and Space Administration (NASA) and other space agencies all over the world wanted to take this opportunity to study the Sun's activities as they built up to the Solar Maximum. Two spacecraft, *Ulysses* and the *Solar and Heliospheric Observatory* (*SOHO*) were launched in the early 1990s with plans to still be operating during the Solar Maximum.

The NASA spacecraft *Ulysses* was designed as a joint mission shared by NASA and the European Space Agency (ESA).

Electrical Knock-Out

In 1989, solar flares interrupted electrical service throughout Canada's province of Quebec—an area covering 595,000 square miles (1.5 million sq km).

*An artist's illustration of **SOHO** in space. This hardy spacecraft has been making continuous observations of the solar surface, the Sun's corona, and the solar wind since its launch in 1995.*

It was launched in 1990 from the space shuttle. It set out to study the Sun's polar regions. To put *Ulysses* into the right orbit over the poles of the Sun, NASA sent it first in the opposite direction—to swing by Jupiter! Then the spacecraft used Jupiter's gravity to swing back over the Sun and into a polar orbit. From this lookout, *Ulysses* can observe areas of the Sun never seen before.

Ulysses carries nine instruments and each one measures a different aspect of the Sun. Scientists use these onboard instruments to gain understanding of the solar wind, magnetic fields and particles, interplanetary dust and gas, and cosmic rays. They use radio data gathered by *Ulysses* to study the Sun's corona.

SOHO was launched on December 2, 1995. It makes observations of the ultraviolet (UV) radiation that comes from the Sun. This spacecraft orbits in an unusual spot, between Earth and the Sun at a distance of 932,000 miles (1.5 million km). It hovers at the point where Earth's gravity balances the Sun's. For the first time, *SOHO* gives scientists a long-term, uninterrupted view of the Sun. This ringside seat means that *SOHO* can provide a lot of general information about the Sun.

These spaceborne observatories have enabled scientists to view the Sun in ways never before possible. They carry sophisticated instruments that help unlock the Sun's mysteries. They fly closer to the Sun in regions no one could see from Earth, and they fly high, free of the blur caused by Earth's atmosphere. These and future crafty robots hold many keys to understanding the inner workings of the closest star.

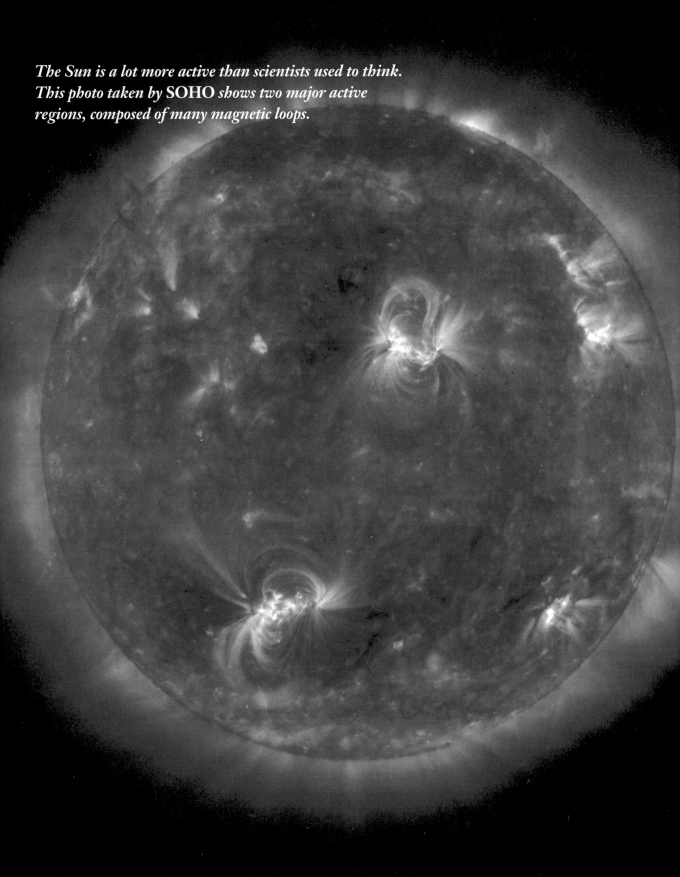

The Sun is a lot more active than scientists used to think. This photo taken by SOHO shows two major active regions, composed of many magnetic loops.

Chapter Five

Getting Hotter or Colder?

In recent years, scientists have discovered that our Sun is less predictable than they once thought. The giant fusion furnace that produces energy in its core could vary its output as much as 1 percent over a long span of time. That doesn't seem like much, but we'd notice the difference.

From the 1500s to the 1700s, a period of extreme cold that people called the

During the "Little Ice Age" in the years 1683 to 1684, people in England held "Frost Fairs" on the frozen waters of the River Thames.

Little Ice Age swept Europe. The River Thames in London froze over, and festivals were even held on the ice. The Thames didn't usually freeze before that, and it has never frozen since. During part of that time, between the years 1645–1715, people observed fewer sunspots than usual on the Sun's surface. Some scientists conclude that the Sun's brightness also may have dimmed for about 200 years.

Scientists currently estimate that the Sun is about 4.5 billion years old and has used up only about half the hydrogen fuel in its core. Fossil records show that life began on Earth almost 4 billion years ago. Scientists estimate that the Sun can support life for at least another 5 billion years.

Warming Sun?

Still, some scientists who study the environment have noticed that the weather on Earth seems to be getting warmer. The ice caps at the poles and glaciers are beginning to melt. Many environmentalists think this warming is caused by human activity. Our use of fossil fuels—fuels we get from Earth, such as natural gas, coal, and oil—contributes to the carbon dioxide in the atmosphere. Exhaust from cars, trucks, and factory smokestacks is contributing to these changes in Earth's environment. These fumes contain large amounts of carbon dioxide, a gas that traps the Sun's heat. This gas lets the Sun's infrared radiation in to warm Earth, but doesn't let the warmth radiate back out. It works in much the same way as glass windows do in a greenhouse. This is known as a greenhouse effect. The Sun's warmth can get trapped beneath the atmosphere's blanket of carbon dioxide and can be unable to escape.

Some scientists think that an increase in carbon dioxide in Earth's atmosphere will lead to increased global temperatures. The red coloring in this computer-generated model shows areas that would have the highest temperature increase if carbon dioxide in Earth's atmosphere was doubled.

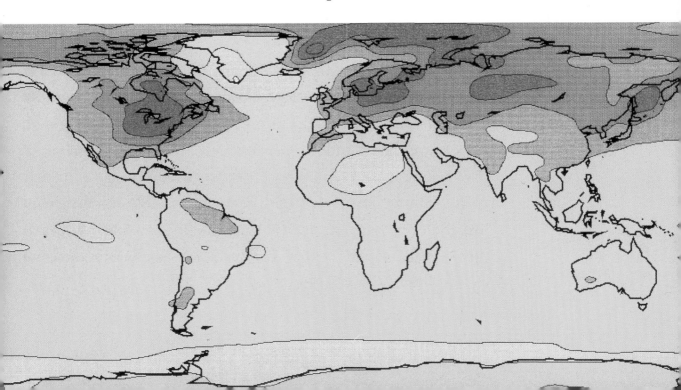

A group of scientists has observed that over a 20-year period the temperature on Earth dropped every time disturbances on the Sun became more intense. On the other hand, when solar magnetism drops off and holes in the Sun's corona get bigger, temperatures on Earth seem to rise. Some scientists believe Earth's climate may be warming up too much as a result of these influences.

When the Sun Dies

Eventually, when the Sun uses up all the hydrogen in its core, it will begin the final stage of a star's evolution. The release of nuclear energy will stop. The energy balance it has maintained for billions of years will come to an end. The core will contract and become even hotter.

If enough heat is generated in the core, nuclear reactions may start up again. The shell of the star would inflate, probably extending beyond Earth. Then it would cool, instantly becoming a **red giant**.

If nuclear reactions do not start up again, the Sun's outer layers will expand more slowly, becoming cooler and brighter. After 6.5 billion years, the Sun will be a huge, swelling orange disk more than 3 times its present size. It will boil away all of Earth's oceans and completely destroy its atmosphere. At that point, life on Earth will no longer be possible. Later, it will expand even more, up to 100 times its present size. Its atmosphere will extend farther outward, eventually surrounding both Mercury and Venus.

In old age, the Sun may continue to consume the heavier elements now existing in its core. It will continue to collapse, becoming hotter and hotter, and denser and denser. Finally the material will become so dense it can no longer contract. It may glow faintly for a while, as a **white dwarf**. All its outer layers will be gone, and our star will shrink to about the size of Earth.

Finally, the last of the Sun's glow will go out, and it will become what astronomers call a **black dwarf**—a cold, dark, lifeless cinder. The remaining planets and their moons will no longer be visible in the icy blackness that surrounds the Sun, but they will continue to follow their lonely orbits.

The star Betelgeuse, shown in the center of this picture, is a red giant.

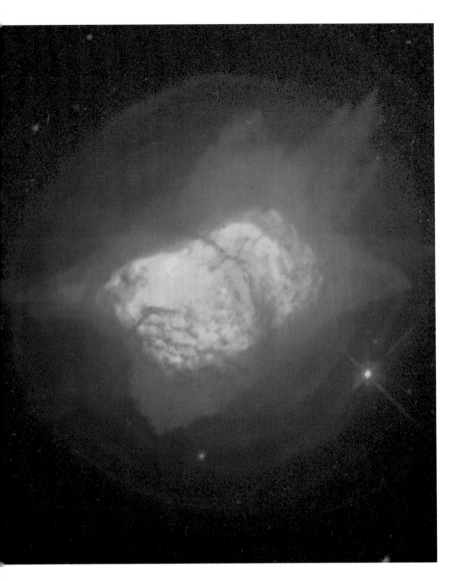

This fate, however, is billions and billions of years in the future. Long before the Sun dies—before the Sun has become too hot for comfort—humans will have had time to make changes. It is possible that we will have developed the technology to leave Earth for another, safer home somewhere else in the universe!

In the meantime, the Sun's influence on Earth and the rest of the solar system offers a small piece of an even larger puzzle. By learning about the Sun and its relationship to the solar system, we can come to understand more about the universe we live in. We can find out more about the great principles of physics that govern the universe, the history of its stars and other star-planet systems, and the many other mysteries and secrets we have not yet discovered.

This image of a dying star was taken by the Hubble Space Telescope in 1996.

Glossary

asteroid—a large piece of rock that orbits the Sun and formed at the same time as the Sun and planets

atmosphere—the gases that surround a planet or other body in space.

atom—the smallest unit of an element (such as hydrogen)

aurora borealis—colorful display caused by the interaction of the solar wind with Earth's atmosphere and magnetic field

axis—the imaginary line running from pole to pole through a planet's center. A planet spins, or rotates, along its axis.

black dwarf—a star at the end of its evolution, when it has completely exhausted its fuel and is cold, small, dense, and dark

chromosphere—a thin region of the Sun between the corona and the photosphere

comet—a small ball of rock and ice that orbits the Sun. When a comet approaches the Sun, some of the ice melts and releases gases. These gases form a tail behind the comet.

convective zone—one of the inner layers of the Sun, located between the radiative zone and the photosphere

core—the distinct region that is located at the center of a star or other object in space

corona—a massive region of gases extending far out from the Sun; the source of the solar wind

equator—an imaginary line around the center of a sphere, such as the Sun or Earth

gravity—the force that pulls objects toward the center of the Sun, a planet, or other body in space

magnetic field—the area around a magnet that is affected by its force

magnetism—the force of a magnet that enables it to attract certain objects from a distance

mass—the amount of material a body contains

nuclear fusion—the reaction that takes place when light atomic nuclei (the central portions of atoms) combine to form a heavier nucleus with the release of energy

orbit—the path an object, such as a planet, travels as it revolves around another body, such as the Sun

photon—a tiny packet of electromagnetic energy, such as light. A photon has no mass, no charge, and an unknown lifetime.

photosphere—the "surface" of the Sun—the area of the Sun that we see

protostar—a very young star, at the beginning of its formation

radiative zone—one of the inner layers of the Sun, located just above the Sun's core

red giant—an enormous, very bright star that has a low surface temperature for a star

revolve—to move in a path, or orbit, around another object. Earth revolves around the Sun, making a complete trip in one year.

rotate—to turn or spin around a central point

solar flare—a sudden, highly explosive burst of light and energy on the surface of the Sun

solar nebula—a cloud of gas and material from which the Sun and the planets were born

solar wind—a stream of highly magnetic particles that flows at high speeds from the Sun's surface

white dwarf—an old star, toward the end of its evolution, often white, usually very dense, small, and faint

To Find Out More

Books

The news from space changes fast, so it's always a good idea to check the copyright date on books to make sure that you are reading current information.

Campbell, Ann Jeanette. *The New York Public Library Amazing Space: A Book of Answers for Kids*. New York: John Wiley & Sons, 1997.

Estalella, Robert, and Marcel Socias. *Our Star—The Sun*. Hauppauge, N.Y.: Barron's Educational Series, Inc., 1993.

Gallant, Roy A. *When the Sun Dies*. New York: Marshall Cavendish, Inc., 1998.

Gardner, Robert. *Science Project Ideas about the Sun.* Springfield, N.J.: Enslow Publishers, Inc., 1997.

Kosek, Jane Kelly. *What's Inside the Sun?* New York: The Rosen Publishing Group, Inc., 1999.

Sorensen, Lynda. *Sun.* Vero Beach, Fla.: Rourke Corporation, 1993.

Vogt, Gregory L. *The Solar System: Facts and Exploration.* Scientific American Sourcebooks. New York: Twenty-First Century Books, 1995.

CD-ROM

Beyond Planet Earth
For Macintosh and PC (DOS, Windows, OS2). From the Discovery Channel School Multimedia. An interactive journey through the solar system. Includes video from NASA and *Voyager* missions and more than 200 photographs. Discovery Channel School, P.O. Box 970, Oxon Hill, MD 20750-0970

Video

Discover Magazine: Solar System
Discovery Channel School, P.O. Box 970, Oxon Hill, MD 20750-0970

Organizations and Online Sites

These organizations and groups are good sources of information about the Sun and the other objects of the solar system. Many of the online sites listed below are NASA sites, with links to many other interesting sources of information.

NASA Ask a Space Scientist
http://image.gsfc.nasa.gov/poetry/ask/askmag.html#list
Interactive page where NASA scientists answer your questions about astronomy, space, and space missions.

The Nine Planets: A Multimedia Tour of the Solar System
http://www.seds.org/nineplanets/nineplanets/nineplanets.html
Includes excellent material on the Sun, created by the Students for the Exploration and Development of Space, University of Arizona

Planetary Missions
http://nssdc.gsfc.nasa.gov/planetary/projects.html
Page of NASA links to all current and past missions, a one-stop shopping center to a wealth of information

The Planetary Society
65 North Catalina Avenue
Pasadena, CA 91106-2301
http://www.planetary.org/

Sky Online

http://www.skypub.com

The web site for *Sky and Telescope* magazine and other publications of Sky Publishing Corporation. This site has a good weekly news section on general space and astronomy news. The site also contains many good tips for amateur astronomers, as well as a nice selection of links. A list of science museums, planetariums, and astronomy clubs organized by state helps locate nearby places to visit, as well.

Welcome to the Planets

http://pds.jpl.nasa.gov/planets/

Tour of the solar system with a lot of pictures and information. Created by California Institute of Technology for NASA/Jet Propulsion Laboratory.

Windows to the Universe

http://windows.arc.nasa.gov/

NASA site, developed by the University of Michigan, includes sections on "Our Planet," "Our Solar System," "Space Missions," and "Kids' Space." Choose from presentation levels of beginner, intermediate, or advanced. To begin exploring, go to the URL above and choose "Enter the Site."

A Note on Sources

When we write about space science, we like to find the most up-to-date sources we can because scientists keep finding out more and more about the universe. We read as many of the latest books as we can find. (You should see our library—wall-to-wall books!) We find recent articles in science magazines such as *Scientific American* and *Science News*. We also use the Internet a lot. The National Aeronautics and Space Administration (NASA) keeps us up-to-date by e-mailing us the latest reports from scientists who study the data from spacecraft. We also check the NASA web pages (such as those listed at the end of this book). Our favorite kind of research involves talking with solar and planetary scientists about what they love best—the work they are doing to discover more about our solar system and the universe.

We would especially like to thank Sam Storch, lecturer at the American Museum-Hayden Planetarium, who reviewed the manuscript and made many excellent suggestions. Finally, a special thank you to our patient editors—Tara Moncrief, who oversaw production and helped us immensely, and Melissa Stewart, who supplied us with a steady stream of clippings on news about the Sun.

—*Ray Spangenburg and Kit Moser*

Index

Numbers in *italics* indicate illustrations.

About the Authors

Ray Spangenburg and Kit Moser write together about science and technology. This husband-and-wife writing team has written 38 books and more than 100 articles. Their works include a five-book series on the history of science and a series on space exploration and astronomy. Their writing has taken them on some great adventures. They have flown on NASA's Kuiper Airborne Observatory (a big plane carrying a telescope). They have also visited the Deep Space Network in the Mojave Desert, where signals from spacecraft are collected. They have even flown in zero gravity on an experimental NASA flight. Ray and Kit live and write in Carmichael, California, with their two dogs, Mencken (a Sharpei mix) and F. Scott Fitz (a Boston Terrier).